TICKING

Stephen Brooke

Eggshell Boats 2022

Ticking
©2022 Stephen Brooke and the Arachis Press

All rights reserved. The text, art and design of this publication are the copyrighted work of Stephen Brooke and the Arachis Press and may not be reproduced nor transmitted in any form without the express written permission of the author or publisher, other than short quotes for review purposes.

ISBN 978-1-937745-82-0

Eggshell Boats
is an imprint of the Arachis Press

Arachis Press
4803 Peanut Road
Graceville, FL 32440
http://arachispress.com

TICKING

Stuff

Stuff happens. We make of it
what we will, lessons,
meanings, fate. What matter

if it is all truly
random? So what if God
hands you only the unformed

stuff of life, says mold it
as you can, fashion
of it as you will?

I'll give you no reasons
why today is as
it is and yesterday,

a discarded lump
of clay. So is life shaped
between our clumsy fingers.

Ticking

When each of us contains our own
end-times, rising from the grave
of self, can time be but the ticking
of a bomb? Hear the clocks,
their steady mechanisms marking
monotony till we no longer
note our passage into nothing.

   background in focus
   but the faces are blurred ~
   an old memory

Instant

I keep a box of memories
in the pantry of my mind.
Just pull one out, add ink and stir
for instant poetry.

And on those days
their taste may seem
a tad too bitter-sweet to swallow
I just recall I paid for each,

paid so long ago,
and shouldn't let them go to waste.

Give and Take
a simple song

Laugh when you are happy,
cry when you are sad;
rejoice in what you have,
remember what you had.
Life will give and take
and life will go on;
night will follow sunset,
day will follow dawn.

Now is but a border
drawn on the map of time,
dividing all that is,
an ever restless line.
Dividing what once was
from what is to be;
no one can live there,
not you, no, not me.

I've turned life inside out
to know its emptiness;
if there's something more
is anybody's guess.
The sun shines ever on,
though we hope and fear;
you'll see it rise tomorrow—
I may not be here.

Snare

Tomorrow is the trap placed
cunningly in our path.

We can not help stepping
into it. Rabbits in the snare,

we hang awaiting our fate.

Accretion

Not one of us is ever
complete. Add more. Add
another piece and measure
against infinity.

I grow, accreting all
this debris of life.
In time I could become
planets, stars unnumbered,

a universe and still
fall short. No matter. Time
has not the length to make
me whole and at the end

each piece will fall away.

Ashtrays

Seven ashtrays, passed from one generation
of nonsmokers to the next—they have held
candy and nick-knacks and paper clips.
They have been ornaments on coffee tables.

The green one is ugly. I know that.
A mottled trilobite, the ceramic chic
of another generation, it squats
unused. It makes a comfortable clutter.

This one might look good over there or maybe
in the other room. Does it matter?
They might sit here or they might all sit in boxes
until someone else will find them as useless as I.

In Between

There was a beginning
and there will be an end.

A big bang and a slow
dissolution.

Aren't we lucky to be
living in between?

Spring Comes

Spring comes when it will:
it cares not for the plans of we
who write down dates on paper.

'Now it's time for Spring,'
we say, and measure our short lives
against eternal heaven's

wheel of stars. But I
hear Spring, this fitful fading night
of Winter's end, and waken:

Spring comes when it will,
a bird song at the dawn,
a soft breeze from the South.

Valentine

Why must I ever be thus halting and unsure,
In fear my words will find their birth come premature?
Our friendship has grown steady strong, it will endure,
But has yours grown, as mine, into a love now pure?

Your presence seems to me a draught of heady wine;
My hopes all whisper of the day you might be mine.
Come fill my dreams, my heart, I but await some sign;
Come be my love, come ever be my valentine.

V-Day

Of course, I could be in love. It happens,
has happened before. But you know me,
I'm the cautious guy. I'm the guy who has
to be sure before he hands over his heart

and even then, ah, even then it has
been handed back once or twice. No different
than you, right? So here comes that day again,
that almost-Spring hearts-and-candy day,

when I suppose I should say something and maybe
mean it. Or maybe not; if any day was right
to test the waters of romance, it's this one.
I'll buy a card or three and throw them in.

Something ventured—but not too much—
and something gained, perhaps. And my heart?
I could hand it over some other day, lace trimmed
and pasted on crimson paper.

   The red-bud announces the spring.
   Will love also show
   it's colors?

Wine and Chocolate

Must I ply you with wine
To make you my Valentine?
Or does it take chocolate too?
I could buy a box for you.

But don't go asking for jewelry;
I can't afford the tomfoolery
of baubles and trinkets and such
and know I haven't the touch

for romance of any sort
or the paying of court.
Heck, it's even hard
to choose a Valentine card!

I'd say *humbug* but remember
I did that back in December;
so I'll just forget the day;
tomorrow it all goes away.

   fragrant snowflakes drift
   upon a springtime breeze ~
   pear blossom blizzard

Martyr

Valentine was a martyr but not
a martyr for love, unless one counts
love of God, which has its own perks
but isn't quite the same. I do

not doubt that he knew earthly love
as well, no matter quite how holy
a saint he might have been. I do
not doubt that he was human as I.

Valentine never shared a box
of chocolates but I'm sure he would
have enjoyed it. I could see
him chewing a nougat as he composed

serious letters of hope, despite
prison walls about him, death
ahead. The season of his feast day
and his letter writing made

of him a saint of paper hearts,
a saint of lovers and of every
martyr with an empty mailbox.
Valentine would write each of them

a message of hope, if he could.

An April Fool

When days are warm but nights still cool
I'm just another April fool,
Listening for the first soft calls
of Chuck-will's-widow as dusk falls
across the firefly-lit fields.

In March, as stubborn Winter yields
reluctantly to Spring's advances,
life awakens and then dances,
dances like an April fool,
a carefree lad, cutting school.

And wind-blown flowers beside a pool,
in mirrored motley, as a fool,
dance as well to vernal song—
those strains, so distant and yet strong,
I recall from Springs afore.

Now I'll join in that song once more,
when berries blossom along the fence.
If in these days, I make no sense
just know me for an April Fool;
I'm but another April fool.

   camellias fade
   as azaleas blossom ~
   birds build nests in both

Fancy

Where a young man's fancy turns
this time of year, we know;
what about a fellow such
as me? Might I sow
the few wild oats I set aside
(for I've frugal ways)?
I can not fling them quite so far
as in my youthful days!

Perhaps I am not yet too old
and, after all, it's Spring;
nothing ventured, as they say,
will surely nothing bring.
Now's the time to once more blossom,
before I go to seed,
before they plant me 'neath the earth,
far beyond all need!

Where a young man's fancy turns
this time of year, turns mine,
but I've become religious now,
knowing love's divine,
and worship with a seriousness
lacking long ago;
if only I as a young man
knew what I now know!

Dance

Soon enough, we will hear the Chuck-wills-widow
sing its solo over a tree frog chorus.

We will see the fire-flies hang lanterns in the trees,
all in preparation for Summer's dance.

We've been invited once again this year.

>   blackberries~
>   spring ripens into summer
>   along each fence row

All I Planted

I've rarely seen a sky so blue,
or mornings with so little dew—
the low humidity's the cause,
and as drought's hungry edge now gnaws
at all I planted new this year,
I hope the rainy season's near.

For all I planted in the Spring,
that came up green and promising,
and wore the season as its gown,
has withered with me, turning brown.
The sky's too blue, and very clear;
I pray the rainy season's near.

Bones

You have become bleached islands,
hidden in a mist of green and brown.

Last spring, I would look away;
you were a stench at road side.

Will your bones still say deer
next summer, amid the high grasses?

> summer day ~
> glasses slide down
> my nose

> Jove's distant rockets
> rumbled long after mortals
> called it a day

> last chrysanthemum
> bows its head to the frost ~
> summer abdicates

falling leaves
hide the grass I left
unmowed

November night ~
a nip in the air
and in my cup

Turkey

Thanksgiving is a turkey
of a holiday,
isn't it? I mean,
no gifts, no candy,
just a big old bird
and football games. I'm over
the river and through the woods
and out of here, Grandma.

flower and bee flew
away on winter's winds ~
honey is still sweet

winter rain ~
seed catalogs and naps
fill the day

shepherds count
the winter stars ~
an angel sings

Behold

Behold the fading of another year:
Though night grows long and dark, be of good cheer.
The celebration of his birth draws near,
The birth of he who came to end our fear.

As shepherds simple in a field once gazed
Upon the star that high above them blazed,
So we may hear the angels' voices raised
And stand with them before the one they praised.

This yuletide, take a moment to recall,
As you may trim your tree and deck your hall,
He who was humbly born in stable stall;
A merry Christmas I wish one and all.

Christmas lights
dance on the house
for those who pass by;
it is dark inside.

Dawn and Dark

Tomorrow brings both dawn and dark,
and all the hours that lie between
will come and go. The bird will build
its nest. It sings to sun and moon.

My heart yet lingers in the valley,
among the sighing trees, among
the shadows where we said goodbye
when yesterday brought dawn and dark.

The young birds hatch and fly away,
returning with the season's change;
Too many dawns await before
I hear their song and see your face.

Crow

The neighbor's chickens
do not greet the new day.
They crow because they must crow.
They crow because they are chickens
and do not count the days.
I do. I greet the new day
when the chickens crow—
when the neighbor's chickens
crow because they must crow.

Waiting

Today's flavor is as bland
as what was served yesterday.

The crowd *oohs* and *aahs* over the change,
opening their empty wallets.

Would there be any point
in waiting for tomorrow?

   the pendulum swings
   and swings back again ~
   the clock ticks on

Janus

Janus-faced Life, I think I know you
until you turn your head. You sing
your own harsh harmony, and which
is the tune and which counterpoint?

Look both ways, god of beginnings
and of ends. Look for me
on the road as I plod toward somewhere
else. It is beyond those hills

where even you cannot see.

Prayer-Book

Hold up your hands that they
might be my true prayer-book.
I will read there my matins,
my lauds, my vespers, words

of praise and supplication.
Before I sleep, as I
begin each day, I'll pray,
and you—you shall be heaven.

To you, I raise my eyes.
In you, I seek the day,
in every page, in all
the hours of my office.

And when this book of you
I finish, each prayer spoken,
believed, there waits the church
my heart has longed to enter.

I will, and worship, find
within your hallows all
in daily prayers I've asked,
read from my true prayer-book.

Erosion

Each lover we thought we needed,
without whom we could not live,
fades. Day by day, year after year,
the memories erode, crumble into
the river of time and are washed
away. What sea holds them all?

   Our brief love
   divided my life
   In two.

Wife

Life's a love affair,
a girl's sunny smile,
the dalliance of a day,

and Death's the wife who waits
while we have our fling.

Waits behind her shuttered
windows for we who have
philandered with the light,

when Life inevitably
turns to her next lover.

The Soil

The mansion does not care who built it
nor the field who worked along
its rows. The trees forget the past,
standing silent by the way,
each year as the one before,
each memory gone with its season.

No ghosts linger—those we bring
in our own battered boxes, those
our mothers and our fathers taped
closed, pretended to forget.
We've pulled them from the closet dark
but dared not break the brittle seals.

Hear them sing into this morning
as they are released. The pains
and joys of yesterday must mingle
in an uncertain haze of distance.
Tomorrow never holds all we
pour into it. Let the soil

lap it up. The soil forgives
when we can not. The soil forgets
for us, asleep in its embrace,
with each year as the one before,
each memory gone with its season.
The soil cares not who tilled it once.

Drink

We are handed this wonderful poison.
Drink deeply, knowing. Drink deeply of life.
It courses, singing of beginnings

and of ends. It burns. Relief
and pain must mingle in that draught.
Let it work its way into you,

through you, finding some tomorrow
to finish its task. Drink deeply, slowly.
Drink knowing time has time enough.

Echoes

Each name shouted into history
echoes, echoes, returning as
a whisper. Each fades into the white
noise of time, and we ask,

*What was that? Did you hear
something?* A wind, perhaps, to carry
today away, carry us
toward tomorrow and our own echoes.

Only wind, blowing through
the trees, up there on the ridge.
We can go across it tomorrow
and shout into the valley beyond.

Dallas

I don't remember what class
it was, only that it was
mid-afternoon at Saint Catherine's
and a nun came into our eighth-grade
classroom and whispered to our nun
and the world was changed.

And the world went on,
too, and we lived to see
the Beatles on Ed Sullivan
and the war in Vietnam
and every war since, and some
went away and they also died.

If things were different
it was because things are always
different. We changed them
and they changed us and we
marched or married, got
religion or became hippies.

Dallas cast its shadow
but like all shadows it fades
with distance. We can barely
see it from here and soon
it will disappear
into books and blurry videos.

Parade

Outside my window, the nations parade
in martial finery,
to disappear with a fading of drums
and a rustle of pages.

Applaud the polished shields of Rome,
the prancing Arab steeds;
each new spectacle must pass
before the next may march

up the street, around the corner
and away, forgotten.
The street lies long but never empty;
I wait with the crowd.

Shadows

The past lies behind me
  whatever way I turn.
All that once was
  is now hidden.
Is that the moon setting
  on my horizon?
Its shadows fall long
  as do the years.

Hostages

The universe has taken
hostages and made
demands we refuse to meet.

Now, the walls of night
keep out only as much
as they once kept in,

all of nothing. Every
star that knows my fate
has hidden itself at last,

as I let go of the past
and found nothing else
to which I might cling.

It is either belief
or the nihilist's void.
No center ground would hold

my weight. I've grown as heavy
as time, as heavy as
God's hand on heaven's wheel,

all dark energy.
What hope for hostages
in our cold distant endings?

The shabby uniforms
of yesterday are on
parade. Salute their passing.

Mistakes

Trying to avoid
the mistakes of the past
we make the mistakes
of the present.

No worse are they than those
of our fathers, no more
foolish. To err remains
exceedingly human.

Blunder on, muddle
through; our children know
that they will do far better
when their turn comes.

Celebrate

Celebrate. Yes, celebrate
if you will, this one second
among the billions of years
that pass on billions of worlds.
It is your second. You have no other.

Obituary

The girl I had a crush
on in high school.

Beloved mother
and grandmother, I read.

What lay among the fifty years
that passed between?

Back Row

The cut-up in the back of the classroom,
the fool who refuses to learn—
I ignore each of life's lessons,
Never wait my turn.

Oh, and all my friends will laugh,
there in the back row,
each time I open my mouth to prove
just how little I know.

It's too late now to change my grades
or be teacher's pet;
dismissal bell is ringing and I've
only learned regret.

Written

Each memory has turned to words,
fixed its form upon the page.
How might I disagree with what
is written, all in twelve-point truth?

Too late to change a single phrase,
re-remember all that was;
I can only read again,
choosing to believe it so.

These are the lines I wrote to play
my role, the poignant platitudes
attached to every mist of you.
Each word has turned to memory.

One

Another square
on another page
of another calendar~
we number it 'one'
and go on.

On the Page

I am not the words on the page
any more than I am that old picture
of me. After all, we are made
anew every few years, right?

All those words, yes, they were written
by someone else. Sometimes, that once was
hands me one and whispers,
You can do this a bit better—

go ahead, but sign my name to it.
I've no problem collaborating with every me
that ever was and maybe some
to come. We'll all sign the same name.

Age

Time lied about its age,
hiding those two billion

years in hopes we wouldn't
notice. All that is gone,

vanished with a bang.
Yes, of course, a big one.

Where shall we find all those
extra candles next year?

Dark Times

All times are dark times. War and Pestilence
ever ride on our horizons, ragged
Famine behind, her black and tattered cloak
a banner heralding Death. Those thin shadows
linger at the edges of our sunlit
days; they whisper of what was and will be.

All times are dark times. Eyes gleam in the night
beyond the tribal fire. Swords run red,
not caring whose the blood they shed nor whose
the hand that wields them. We forget, forget
too readily, the phantoms of our past,
dismiss the ephemeral dread astir in our souls.

All times are dark times. Sing aubades though night
returns, ever returns. I see the riders
along that distant ridge. Their hoof-beats throb
and fade beneath the din of life, yet grow
inexorably louder. Life has fled
before them, fled through millennia unnumbered,

down into the ebon seas forgotten
of man and time. Let howl the wolves! Draw forth
the sword! We glimpse their advent with the night.
All times are dark times. Come, draw near the fire.
We can only build it high and wait
for the dawn, as we have done before.

The Creation of Time

Then god created the stars
and set his angels to counting them.
It took forever.

It continues to rain.
Each drop speaks its name
and then forgets it.

When the moon waxes,
the birds sing all night,
calling tomorrow home.

I have written out my future,
etched it on the rocks that slowly
erode into nothing.

Who can read it now?
Who could trace the letters
and count the stars

to find her name?

    I would
    not mind wasting
    all my hours, all my days,
    if only that time were wasted
    with you.

Whisper

Of course, this poem is for you—
they all are, you know?

Each word becomes another way
to speak your name.

To whom else would I whisper of love
in hopes of being overheard?

Passion

There must be passion: passion enough to leave
us trembling, leave us weary with delight.
Not need. Not friendship. These, too, can be love;
lives can be built on such, and happiness.

Am I so wrong in seeking more? Are you
then wrong to feel that something must be missing?
Two lonely fools are we and nothing more,
unready to accept less than our dreams.

Now we will press each memory of our love
between the pages of what might have been,
to find one day, breathe in the faded scent
of almost, of our something less than passion.

Land

It requires a fine balance,
this being half-in-love.
We teeter on the easeless
knife edge of maybe
until we must fall one way
or the other, in or out.

Whichever it may be,
it will hurt when we land.

I have built wings of paper,
longer each day. Once, I thought
they would let me fly away,
glide to new skies, set me
on firm ground. Too late.
They have grown unwieldy—

too long, too heavy.
I can only fall the harder.

> I missed you all of yesterday.
> Must I still miss you
> tomorrow?

Real

Love is no more than a word;
I can not hold it in my arms
as I might hold you.

Nor can faith be peeled like an orange,
broken into sections, the juice
seeping sticky through my fingers.

I have tried to live in the towers
we construct. There is no
solid footing at their top.

There is no shelter within their walls.
Love is no more than a word;
You and I, we are real.

Saint

Patient I must be,
so patient I will be.
I'll wear this virtue like
a saint, if saint you seek.

Saint I can be as long
as need be and I
can wait until that day
you can wait no longer.

I must now to my prayers

Questing

To be with you proves one more task,
as I quest for my holy grail.
Had I but known, I might have spoken;
hope's glamour will ensorcell those

who must ride forth, their words all sleeping.
A whispered light along the world's
edge calls me forth to claim this day,
to name this day as ours. I shall,

I must, go questing once again
in you. It leads on to tomorrow,
across rose-tinted yearning dawns
with promise just beyond unreached,

unreachable, horizons. Go,
I tell myself; the quest is not
yet ended, the grail is not yet won.
I've set myself but one more task.

>   Yesterday sings loudly.
>   Will tomorrow ever
>   add harmony?

The Same

To give her up would be too easy.
To let her go, disappear

into another day—the sun
would still shine, would it not?

The rain would still fall. Everything
changes, just as it stays the same,

just as I would stay the same.
I shall not have a past, but live

along the empty roads where time
forgot its way. There, no one

knows her name. I may forget
it myself. Give it a while.

Repairs

I've learned that time, despite all I'd been told,
is not the cure for a broken heart.

We must give it to another,
hand it over for repairs.

No one can put the pieces back together
alone; repair me and I shall repair you.

Flame

I am the same, the flame that danced
once on this candle. I burn more brightly
now, burn more steady. Ah,
but what a fine flickering

I made before. I was full
of shadows, then, and wore the night
in my eyes. The light slipped through
my fingers, leaving only smoke.

I guttered toward my desires,
once, on each breath of wind, in storms
of fitful flame. I faded before
the morning sun's insistent truth.

I have become the day, the burning
song of life. I hold it cupped
within my heart, the flame that is
yet I, this fire that danced once.

   tomorrow crouches
   behind the walls of midnight
   preparing to pounce

Burn

Arsonist, I
burn myself down

tonight. Come
stand by the fire,

and toast s'mores
in my memory.

Sweep Me Up

Sweep me up. I'm ready to go
in your box, be stored away.
My heart's been carried around too long,
been in too many pockets. Sweep me

into your grandfather's cigar
box, the one you've kept for odds
and ends and it's familiar smell,
faded as the memories

you placed there. I will be among them;
just lift the lid, now and again.

Fall

Fall.

Balance wearies,
ever teetering
on the edge
of despair.

Fall forward
and be done.

Fall into
tomorrow, drown
in its promise,
in its darkness.

Fall.

Forget and be
forgotten, be
the meteor
that burned across

some sky and faded,
fallen, fallen.

Lose this balance,
slip away.
Fall to earth,
fall to rest.

Fall.

One Pull
a pantoum

It would not be hard
to put an end to things;
one pull upon the trigger,
then all would fade to darkness.

To put an end to things,
I'd finally take control;
then all would fade to darkness,
then I would find my rest.

I'd finally take control
when life seems only trouble;
Then I would find my rest
in fields of starless night.

When life seems only trouble,
I will yearn for that peace
in fields of starless night,
beyond the reach of sorrow.

I will yearn for that peace;
I someday may yet journey
Beyond the reach of sorrow
and dwell in blessed darkness.

I may someday yet journey:
one pull upon the trigger
and dwell in blessed darkness.
It would not be hard.

Carry Me

I can taste the sweetness
of death. Fill my cup
with that dark wine,
for I thirst.

I can feel the comfort
of earth. Make up my bed,
my deep forever bed,
that I may sleep.

I can hear my own song
fading. Take up the tune,
all you vagrant winds—
carry me.

Carry me away.

Payment

Alas for we who were once counted bold!
Can our forgotten truths be found among
the words now whispered, then more loudly sung,
those fires that burnt hot, now ashes cold?
Why is it men and women must grow old?
It is our payment for once being young.

Healing

Time may heal each wound
but death works even better;
in the earth, cocooned,
be free of every fetter.

Free of want and worry,
free of scam and scheme,
yet I am in no hurry
to sleep, perchance to dream.

Yes, peace comes when we die
and earth is all-forgiving;
but till that time, I'll try—
that's what makes life worth living.

Traveler

Time machines, each of us,
traveling into our unknowable
futures, traveling to meet
those personal Morlocks who dwell
beneath the gardens of our dreams.

No turning back, traveler;
the only control
is the off switch.

To Take Arms

So, is it wrong to take
ones destiny into ones hands,
to make that leap into
the darkness on ones own terms?

I, too, might take arms
against tomorrow, against
insistent fate. Someday,
I may feel the need.

There come days when I
believe, and days I do
not. Which will this be?
Tomorrow speaks too loudly,

and if, in the end,
things have only what meaning
we give, what meaning have we?
Take arms, brother, take arms.

The last day of my life
I may regret all done
and undone. The next day,
I shall not care. Let fall

things as they will; in time,
everything and everyone
is forgotten. Let fall the darkness.
I shall know when to take arms.

One Passing By
a song

Stand around me then,
raise to me one last cup;
toast what we have of life
before we're swallowed up.
And if one passing by
asks whom you lay to rest,
only laugh and tell him,
a fellow of infinite jest.

Let the fife fall silent,
the drum-beat echoes fade;
the mourners will trudge home,
once they have been paid.
And if one passing by
asks who fills this grave,
you need only answer,
one nobody could save.

Now life I'll leave to the living,
whatever border I've crossed;
I never found much worth winning
and even less to be lost.
And if one passing by
asks whom you buried this day,
give him another's name
and send him on his way.

The City of Happiness

It is a name set on a map
I can not read. Beyond what may
be seas or deserts, east or west
of yesterday, it lies. The way
has not been hidden, say the wise;
I need but choose to stand before
its gates to enter. So they say,
but how am I to recognize
that city I have never glimpsed
save in the secrets of your eyes?

   children hurry
     to rebuild sand castles
   as the tide ebbs

Breeze

I have walked with the changeless stars
  and the ever-changing moon,

listening to the calls of distant owls
  fade among the darkened trees.

My poems have no more meaning
  than the breeze in the tops of the pines.

Hard Days

Fill your buckets, fill
your hands. Potatoes are cheap
this year; the fields of famine
lie forgotten. Roadside
they lie, and we walk on.

Bring my finest mare.
Let her blossom here,
into the waiting dust,
ripe with the seed of gods.
Our hard days lie forgotten.

Luggage

We travel with great trains of luggage,
we humans, wherever we check in:
suitcases full of monkeys, bags
with lizards and fish and worms all mixed up

inside. Sometimes the latches fail
and they spill out, crawling away
into corners, swinging from
the curtains, and the concierge

must chase them down, put them back,
lest they upset the other guests.
Slipping out, they might leave all
their luggage by the unmade bed.

Imaginary

You out grew me, your imaginary
friend, left me behind with all the rest

of make believe and childish ways and, *Oh,
I would that you were real*. As do I.

Sleep and dreams are what remain, a closet
of forgetfulness, of frayed sock-monkeys

and princesses. Shall I play the prince
or return to yarn, unraveling

in the darkness? Shut the door; your choices
were all made before you ever found me.

The Future

The future arrived,
neatly wrapped,
this morning.
I picked it up,
gave it a shake
to see if I could tell
what's inside.
I think I broke it.

Hole

Some days this hole goes so deep
I wish someone would come
along and fill it up.

Throw that dirt in, let me
wake on the other side
of forever. Dawn may

remember my name when time
is an empty glass
or maybe night will have

no end but its own.
It tells no one. It only
lets us sleep.

    Only divinity
    can manage infinity;
    the rest of us
    are smaller.

Reality

We're born, we die,
and call those things that lie
between reality.
Might life be but dream?
Might all these things that seem
so urgent now to me
fade as I awake,
each success and mistake
prove naught but mockery,
a fragile moment's light
in the empty night
of eternity?

    Whisper Yesterday's lies
    in Tomorrow's ear.
    She will believe, as always.

    the wind and rain
    erase all history
    given time

One Thousand and One

One thousand and one things
to do today; one thousand
and one and not one of them

names the rising sun.
No, not one is worth
the baptism of dawn.

Bring me tomorrow in
a tall glass and I
shall toast the memories

that were my comrades;
all one thousand and one
and not one worth the keeping.

Waste Not

Waste not, want not, they say
or somebody said. Not anyone
in my family—cliches
were not their thing. It's good
enough advice, I'm sure,
and so I find myself
at the sink, peeling labels
from jelly jars. I will use
them for something, someday,
congratulating myself
for wasting nothing but time.

Naught

We are the glass that one day shatters,
the flame that burns to ash and scatters,
with no regret, for nothing matters.

The little mouse's midnight patters
that, drowsy, we a moment hark
will fade forgotten in the dark.

All leave naught behind to mark
the passage; the igniting spark
dims and dies as we burn yet.

Consume, create, die, beget—
the sun of dawn must also set;
none of it matters—have no regret.

   I spend the days
   playing hide-and-seek
   with myself

   it is my turn
   to close my eyes

Passage

Sing praises of a dying god;
the candles flicker to mark his passage,
the Dow rises and bows in homage,
and his name is lauded all the louder

by the true believer. They all die,
each nation, each god, each comforting
belief, but the dead husks are yet
worshiped for a season or two.

Let the priests hold their noses;
we'll paint lifelike colors on decaying
faces, so they might stare down
with vacant eye upon humanity.

We stare up with no more comprehension.
Everything must go in this final
sale; do not the signs tell us so?
Everything must go and be forgotten.

   sand sifts slowly
   from the broken hourglass
   and is blown away

Tongues

I speak in all the tongues of man,
in hope that you might understand
one word. But one reluctant word
might be enough—is it absurd

to think that so?
I do not know.

It is too much I ask; today
fell from my lips to flow away
and yesterday debates tomorrow
in every language known to sorrow.

I'll not translate,
allowing fate

its course and discourse. I shall seek
some tongue that fallen angels speak,
full of the yearning emptiness
of heaven lost. Could I confess

in full my sin?
I fear the din

of all man's tongues would drown this voice
that learned the words but made no choice.

Twenty-Thousand

I don't mind that God created
time; only that He made
man aware of its steady step
down the road to oblivion.

Twenty-thousand days: is that
enough? Let's roll some dice, Lord,
double or nothing. What have I
got to lose, after all?

Burn On

This brushfire life burns on,
this errant spark that grew
to consume the world.
One blaze extinguished, cold,

another reignited,
enduring, springing up,
a flicker in the darkened
inert universe,

winding down. We burn
a little longer, you
and I. We burn, burn on,
against what night must come.

Join

Being dances eternally
  in the Void.
Do not fear to join
  in for a time
nor to rest when you
  grow tired.

Stars

I have watched the stars grow dim,
one by one, seen them flicker,
at the end, candles snuffed
by the breath of a weary God.

Despair and desire hold hands before
the void, as worlds collapse, as one
cold rock remains, circling some dim
dying ember. Then I, too,

lose my footing, tumble into
inky oblivion. How long
might one fall when time itself
ceases and forever exists

no more? I have plumbed my past
and counted every star that was.

Uncrossed

Beyond the mountains uncrossed,
beyond the blue ocean deep,
will I find all I've given
those I have loved to keep?

Each part of me I've left
behind without one thought;
I would give them freely
for love's not sold nor bought.

And all the years I journeyed,
I knew not what I sought;
yet I am contented
with everything they brought.

The seas roll wide before me,
the mountains rise too steep,
but there my last love waits,
she in whose arms I'll sleep.

Measure

I make a poor yard-stick
but I've no other
to measure the universe

it is bigger than me
and smaller than god.

Count

I'm at the age where I forget my age
and have to count from my birth date
if I can remember what year this is.
No one dwells here to remind me,

no differences appear from one day to
another. Only the mirror tells me
I have changed. It whispers, Look away,
old man. Go find old photos, gray

and faded, gray and faded as you. They once
told a truth of sorts, but posed
on yesterday's stage, a story I could not
believe, even as I told it.

I'm at the age where there is much still to be
done but none of it really matters.
All I can do is shrug, pretending not
to notice. Maybe it never did.

Tomorrow is a little closer each day,
and all these photos are undated,
their age forgotten. I'll not count the years.
None will look at them again.

Who Asks?

Who asks the wind
  why it blows?
Who asks the sun
  why it shines?
Who asks tomorrow
  why it comes?
Be like these.

Epitaph

Where nature is
And the wind blows free,
There bless the ground
And bury me.

a note: *this is my very oldest poem—the oldest I have preserved—written when I was eight*

www.ingramcontent.com/pod-product-compliance
Lightning Source LLC
Chambersburg PA
CBHW051717040426
42446CB00008B/933